My name is

William

I am **2** years old.

My favourite
colour is

Green

Mr Tumble
is funny!

Something Special

Mr Tumble's Annual 2016

Contents

EGMONT
We bring stories to life

First published in Great Britain in 2015 by Egmont UK Limited,
The Yellow Building, 1 Nicholas Road, London W11 4AN

Written by Jane Riordan
Designed by Pritty Ramjee and Claire Yeo
The drawing of Mr Tumble on page 31 is reproduced with thanks to
Jack Henderson of jackdrawsanything.com

SOMETHING SPECIAL™ Copyright © BBC 2004

ISBN 978 1 4052 7898 0
60313/1
Printed in Italy

Hello Mr Tumble!

It's good to see you. Let's have fun together.

You sign
hello

From A to Z with Mr Tumble

Aa
is for apple

Bb
is for Baker Tumble

Cc
is for cake

You sign

cake

Dd
is for dance

Ee
is for egg

Ff
is for Fisherman Tumble

Gg
is for Grandad Tumble

You sign

Grandad

Hh
is for hand

Ii
is for ice

Jj
is for jelly

Kk
is for kite

Ll
is for Lord Tumble

Mm
is for moon

10

Nn
is for nose

You sign

nose

Oo
is for orange

Pp
is for paint

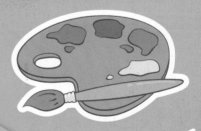

Qq
is for queen

Rr
is for ring

Ss
is for
spotty bag

You sign
spotty bag

Tt
is for tap

Uu
is for umbrella

12

Vv
is for
vegetables

Ww
is for
watering can

Xx
is for x-ray

Yy
is for yo-yo

Zz
is for zip

T for Tumble

Look for all the things in the picture that begin with the **t** sound.

Can you write the ts?

teapot

You say t t t t with Mr Tumble.

tie

teddy

tummy

15

Fisherman Tumble went to sea

★ Sing along!

Fisherman Tumble went to sea, sea, sea

To see what he could see, see, see

But all that he could see, see, see

Was the bottom of the deep blue sea, sea, sea!

You say S S S S with Fisherman Tumble.

16

There is seaweed in the deep blue sea. Join the dots to make more seaweed.

You sign

sea

17

Dotty drawing

Draw over the dots to finish the picture of Mr Tumble!

18

shape play

The Tumbles are playing with shapes! What shapes can you see in the picture?

A little, purple circle!

A red square!

Look for circles when you are out and about.

A big, yellow triangle!

You sign
square

You sign
circle

You sign
triangle

Taking shape

Finish this picture of Mr Tumble's house. You will need to draw squares, a circle, a triangle and two rectangles.

You sign

rectangle

23

Can you see some pink spots?

You sign **green**

You sign **orange**

You sign **pink**

Colourful cooking

These two pictures of Baker Tumble cooking in the kitchen may look the same but some things have changed in picture 2. Can you find the 5 differences?

1

Point to all the red things in the picture!

You sign

red

2

27

Aunt Polly painting

Listen to the story and say the word when you see any of these:

Mr Tumble

Aunt Polly

Red

Yellow

Blue

Green

 was painting a picture of  .

She painted his bright  nose, his

bright  trousers and his

shoes. But she couldn't remember what

colour to paint his waistcoat. Should it be

 ? No, I don't think so. Should

it be ? No, that's not right either.

 's waistcoat is  with

stars!  painted all the stars very carefully. Then she wanted to paint standing by a tree. But she didn't have any paint. What could do?

Clever  mixed the ⬤ and ⬤ paint to make ⬤ . Then she painted a beautiful ⬤ tree with ⬤ apples. What a lovely painting, 🧑 . 🧑 will be pleased.

be pleased.

You could try mixing blue and yellow paint at home.

Colour spinning craft

You will need:
Thin white card
Crayons or pens
Round objects to draw around
Scissors
String

1 Place a cup on the card and draw around it.

2 Cut out the circle with help from an adult.

3 In the middle of your circle draw around a bottle top to make a smaller circle.

4 Cut this out with help from an adult.

5 Now colour your spinning wheel with lots of bright colours.

6 Tie the ends of a length of string together and thread it through the middle of your card.

7 Hold one end of the string in each hand. Swing the string and the colour wheel until the entire length of string is twisted. Then give the string a firm pull and watch it unwind so the colour wheel spins.

★ Why not try: ★

Colour your wheel in stripes of yellow and blue. When the wheel spins you will see green! Your eyes and brain have mixed the blue and yellow together to make green, just like when Aunt Polly mixed the paint!

33

Colour by colour

This picture of Mr Tumble needs much more colour. The small dots will tell you which colours to use.

You sign

colour

34

Count with Mr Tumble

Join in with Mr Tumble and count from 1 to 5.

1
one

Mr Tumble has 1 cake.

37

2 two

Mr Tumble has 2 teddy bears.

3 three

Mr Tumble has 3 balls.

4
four

Mr Tumble has 4 ducks.

5
five

Mr Tumble has 5 flowers.

1 2 3 4 5

Join in with the song, counting on your fingers as you go.

1, 2, 3, 4, 5

Once I caught a fish alive.

6, 7, 8, 9, 10

Then I put it back again.

Why did you let it go?

Because it bit my finger so.

Which finger did it bite?

This little finger on my right!

1
2
3
4
5
6
7
8
9
10

40

41

Gardening time

Look at this picture of Grandad Tumble and his garden shed.

Can you find:

1 watering can

2 wheels

3 clouds

4 flower pots

5 carrots

43

Ice cream parlour

Mr Tumble loves ice cream. You could have your own ice cream parlour and practise your counting at the same time.

You will need:

Coloured paper
A cup
Scissors

1. Place a cup on coloured paper and draw around it.

2. Cut out the circle with help from an adult.

3. Make lots of circles of different colours! Pink for strawberry, white for vanilla, brown for chocolate and organise your ice cream scoops into flavours.

4. Now cut cone-shapes out of brown paper.

5. Serve your ice creams to friends and family and be sure to ask them how many scoops they would like!

44

Why not try?

Cutting out 5 cones and writing the numbers 1 to 5 on them. Then put 1 scoop in the cone marked 1 and so on. Which lucky person will get the cone with 5 scoops in it?

3

4

You sign
1

You sign
2

You sign
3

You sign
4

You sign
5

That hat is too small!

You sign

small

The opposite of long is short.

The opposite of big is small.

Those trousers are too short!

47

Opposite play

Here are some more opposites. Draw a line to link the opposites.

Back

Day

Stop

Happy

Sad

Go

What is the opposite of up? Look for things in your home that are up and things that are down.

Night

Front

What is the opposite of open? Open and close a book.

49

Fun in the cold

Listen to the story and say the word when you see any of these:

happy

sad

hot

cold

50

It was a 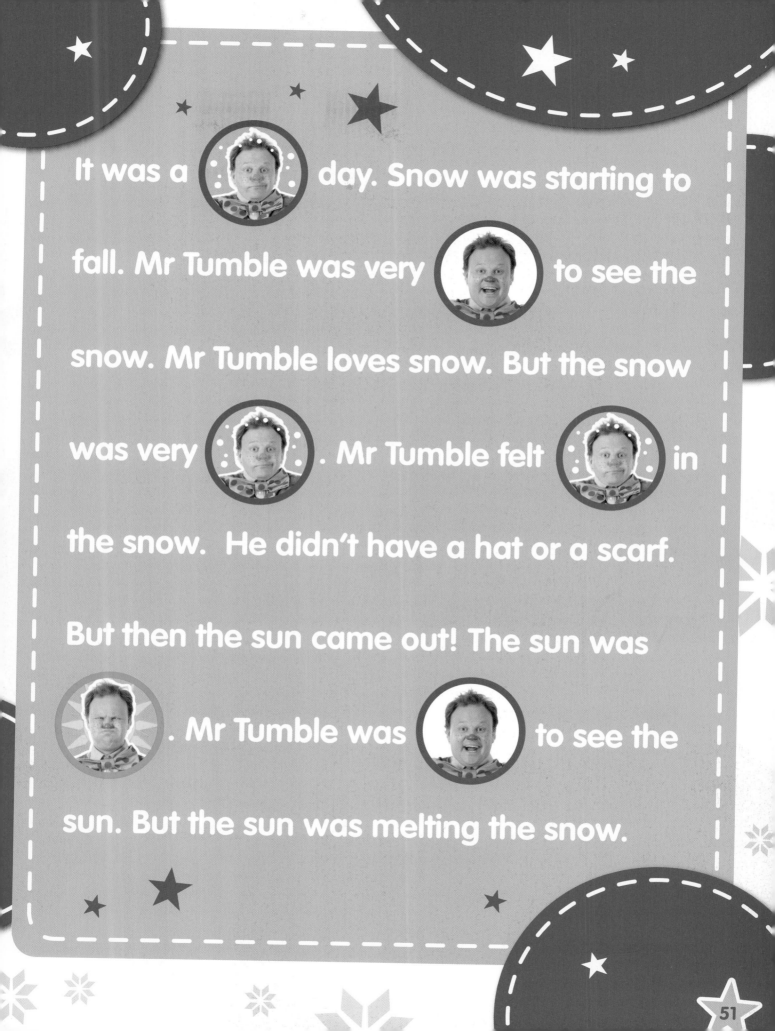 day. Snow was starting to

fall. Mr Tumble was very to see the

snow. Mr Tumble loves snow. But the snow

was very . Mr Tumble felt in

the snow. He didn't have a hat or a scarf.

But then the sun came out! The sun was

. Mr Tumble was to see the

sun. But the sun was melting the snow.

Oh no, Mr Tumble was to see the snow melting. Soon there was no snow left at all. But the next day it snowed again! It was but this time Mr Tumble was ready

with his warm hat and scarf. He was

very  to be able to play in the snow.

Mr Tumble ran through the snow. He made

big snowballs and he drew pictures in the

snow. Mr Tumble was very indeed!

Did you spot any opposites in this story? What is the opposite of hot?

You sign

hot

You sign

cold

Up and down

Colour in this picture of Mr Tumble jumping UP and DOWN.

Can you jump like Mr Tumble?

Something Special

Up

up

and away

with the Tumbles!

Aunt Polly flying high

Colour in this floaty picture of Aunt Polly!

57

Box antics

Mr Tumble is funny and loves to play. Just look how much fun he can have with one box!

Mr Tumble is **under** the box.

Mr Tumble is **on top** of the box.

Mr Tumble is
behind
the box.

Colour the egg **inside** the egg cup orange. Colour the egg **outside** the egg cup blue.

Can you play a game with one of your toys? Try putting it **on top of, under, inside** and **behind** something.

59

Hide-and-seek

All the Tumbles love hiding. Today they're in the park and they're all hiding behind things.

Can you find:

Mr Tumble

Aunt Polly

Baker Tumble

Lord
Tumble

Fisherman
Tumble

Grandad
Tumble

When you find
them wave
and cheer!

The lost teddy

Listen to the story and say the words when you see any of these:

Mr Tumble

Grandad Tumble

teddy

bed

toys

It was bedtime.  brushed his

teeth and climbed into . But

he couldn't find his .

 couldn't sleep without his .

Where could it be? First he looked under

his , but all he found was a sock!

Then he looked inside all his cupboards.

Lots of  came crashing down, but no (teddy). Then (man) looked behind the curtains. He found some more (skittles/ball), but not (teddy). Poor (man) climbed into (bed). He would have to sleep without his (teddy) tonight. But just then there was a knock at the door. It was (man in hat). "Does this fluffy (teddy) belong to you?" he asked. And from behind his back (man in hat) pulled out (man)'s

! "He was hiding inside my shed!"

laughed .  and  were

very pleased to see each other and slept

very well that night!

Do you have a favourite toy at bedtime?

Mr Tumble sat on the wall

Join in with the song to the tune of Humpty Dumpty. Why not make up your own actions to the rhyme?

Colour in the sun **up** in the sky and the flowers **down** on the ground.

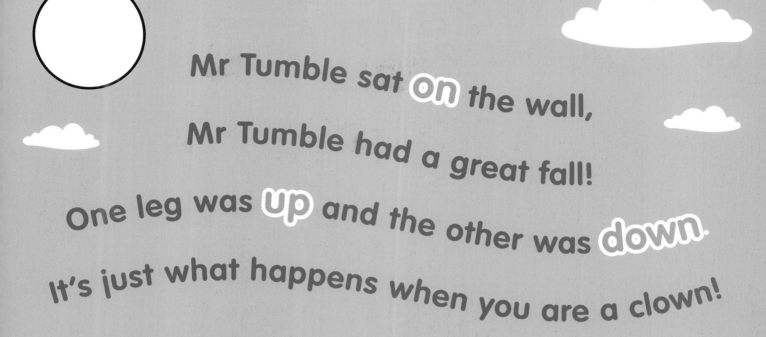

Mr Tumble sat on the wall,
Mr Tumble had a great fall!
One leg was up and the other was down.
It's just what happens when you are a clown!

Goodbye Mr Tumble

Colour in Mr Tumble and wave goodbye. We've had lots of fun today!

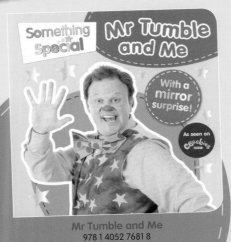